NOTE

T HIS work was originally designed for broadcasting. For concert a ....ations are necessary.

This is especially the case in the accompaniment to the Speaker's voice. For broadcasting, this should be performed *poco forte*, but ' faded down' so as to form a background to the voice. In the concert room this must be represented by the softest *pianissimo* so that the Speaker's voice may absolutely dominate.

The soprano part should be sung by a powerful dramatic voice, but there must be no *vibrato*. On no account should the part be sung by a single boy's voice, though in the case of necessity it may be sung by several boys' voices in unison.

The children's part must be sung by real children's voices, not sophisticated choir boys.

The work was originally scored for large orchestra including six trumpets and six clarinets. If necessary, trumpets 4, 5, and 6 and clarinets 4, 5, and 6 may be omitted and, to meet the needs of even smaller resources, the score has been extensively 'cued in.'

Owing to the chronic scarcity of tenors, the tenor line should be strengthened by a few high baritones. Where the tenor line divides, the higher notes should be taken by the real tenors and the lower by the baritones.

ORCHESTRATION
(Reduced Version)

Flutes 1 & 2	Trombones 1, 2 & 3
Oboes 1 & 2	Tuba (ad lib)
Clarinets 1 & 2	Timpani 2 (or 3)
Bass Clarinet (ad lib)	*may be doubled if another player is available*
Bassoons 1 & 2	Percussion (1 Player)
Double Bassoon (ad lib)	*Side Drum, Triangle, Cymbals, Bass Drum*
Horns 1 & 2	Harp or Piano (ad lib)
Horns 3 & 4 (ad lib)	Organ (ad lib)
Trumpets 1 & 2	*If no Organ, the orchestra should play all Organ cues.*
Trumpet 3 (ad lib)	Strings

(Score and Parts available for Rental)

DURATION 15–16 minutes

A SONG OF THANKSGIVING

SOPRANO SOLO AND CHORUS

Blessed art thou, O Lord God of our fathers; and to be praised and exalted above all for ever.

And blessed is thy glorious and holy Name; and to be praised and glorified above all for ever.

Blessed art thou in the temple of thine holy glory; and to be praised and exalted above all for ever.

Blessed art thou on the glorious throne of thy kingdom, and to be praised and glorified above all for ever.

—Song of the Three Holy Children, vv. 29, 30, 31 & 33

SPEAKER

O God, thy arm was here,
and not to us, but to thy arm alone
ascribe we all. Take it, God, for it is none but thine.

—Henry V, Act IV, Sc. 8.

CHORUS

Thine, O Lord, is the greatness, and the power and the glory.
Thine is the victory, and the majesty; for all that is in the heaven and earth is thine.
Thine is the kingdom, O Lord, and thou art exalted as head above all.

—I Chronicles XXIX, v. 2.

SOPRANO SOLO

O give thanks unto the Lord because he is gracious:
for his mercy endureth for ever.

—Song of the Three Holy Children, v. 67

SPEAKER AND CHORUS

The Spirit of the Lord God is upon me, because the Lord hath anointed me to proclaim liberty to the captives and the opening of the prison to them that are bound, to comfort all that mourn; to give them beauty for ashes, the oil of joy for mourning, the garment of praise for the spirit of heaviness.

—Isaiah, LXI, vv. 1, 2, 3

CHORUS

Go through, go through the gates, prepare ye the way of the people; cast up, cast up the highway; gather out the stones.
Lift up a standard for the people.
Behold, the Lord hath proclaimed unto the ends of the world,—say ye, "Behold thy salvation cometh, Behold, his reward is with him and his work before him."
And they shall call them the holy people, the redeemed of the Lord: and thou shalt be called "Sought Out," a city not forsaken.

—Isaiah, LXII, vv. 10, 11, 12

SPEAKER

And they shall build the old wastes, they shall raise up the former desolations.
And they shall repair the waste cities, the desolations of many generations.

—Isaiah, LXI, v. 4

SPEAKER

    Violence shall be no more heard in thy land,
    wasting nor destruction within thy borders;
    but thou shalt call thy walls Salvation, and thy gates Praise.

CHORUS

    But thou shalt call thy walls Salvation, and thy gates Praise.

—Isaiah, LX, v. 18

CHILDREN'S VOICES

    Land of our birth, we pledge to thee
    Our love and toil in the years to be;
    When we are grown and take our place
    As men and women with our race.

    Father in Heaven who lovest all,
    O help thy children when they call.
    That they may build from age to age
    An undefiled heritage.

CHORUS

    Teach us the strength that cannot seek,
    by deed, or thought, to hurt the weak;
    That, under thee, we may possess
    Man's strength to comfort man's distress.

    Teach us delight in simple things,
    The mirth that has no bitter springs;
    Forgiveness free of evil done,
    And love to all men 'neath the sun.

ALL VOICES

    Land of our birth, our faith, our pride,
    For whose dear sake our fathers died;
    O Motherland, we pledge to thee,
    Head, heart and hand through the years to be.

—Rudyard Kipling*

SOPRANO SOLO

    The Lord shall be thine everlasting light,
    and the days of thy mourning shall be ended.

—Isaiah LX. v. 20

---

*Reprinted from "PUCK OF POOK'S HILL" by permission of Mrs. George Bambridge.

A Song of Thanksgiving

R. VAUGHAN WILLIAMS

OXFORD UNIVERSITY PRESS • NEW YORK AND LONDON

CHORUS
SOPRANO ② ff

And bless-ed is thy glori-ous and ho-ly

ALTO ff

And bless-ed is thy glori-ous and ho-ly

TENOR, BARITONE & BASS ff *

And bless-ed is thy glori-ous and ho-ly

Organ
ff

S.
Name; and to be praised and glo-ri-fied a-bove all for ev-er.

A.
Name; and to be praised and glo-ri-fied a-bove all for ev-er.

T.
Bar.
B.
Name; and to be praised and glo-ri-fied a-bove all for ev-er.

* Upper stems, Tenor and high Baritone

6

Sop. Solo: Bless-ed art thou in the tem-ple of thine ho - ly glo - ry;

Trombone

Sop. Solo: and to be praised and ex - alt - ed a - bove all for ev - er.

③ CHORUS

S. A.: Bless - ed art thou on the glo - rious throne of thy king - dom,

T. Bar.: Bless - ed art thou on the glo - rious throne of thy king - dom,

B.: Bless - ed art thou on the glo - rious throne of thy king - dom,

8

To be spoken— the notation is purely conventional and does not imply any particular pitch, and need not be in absolute strict time, but must finish at the places where the Orchestra and Chorus swell up.

*This is only a 'safety' pause. If the speaker has already reached the last word then go on at once to the next bar.

Sop. Solo: gra - cious: for his mer - cy en - dur - eth for ev - er.

Andante sostenuto ♩= 64 SPEAKER

The Spi-rit of the Lord God is up - on me,

(Organ) p

Piano

Andante sostenuto ♩= 64
(Strings)

pp

Ped.

Spk.: be-cause the Lord hath an - oint - ed me to pro - claim li-ber-ty to the captives

Ped.

SOPRANO & ALTO

pre - pare ye the way of the peo-ple; cast up, cast up the

pre - pare ye the way of the peo-ple;

high - way; ga - ther out the stones.

Lift up a stan-dard for the peo-ple.

Lift up a stan-dard for the peo-ple.

Lift up a stan-dard for the peo-ple.

S.
A.
-hold, his re-ward is with him and his work be-fore him? And they shall

T.
Bar.
And they shall

B.
And they shall

S.
A.
call them the ho - ly peo-ple, the ho -

T.
Bar.
call them the ho - ly peo - ple, the ho -

B.
call them the ho - ly peo - ple, the ho -

8va Bass ad lib.

S.
A.
unis.
- ly peo-ple, the redeemed of the Lord: ____

T.
Bar.
- ly peo-ple, the redeemed of the Lord: ____

B.
- ly peo-ple, the redeemed of the Lord: ____

con 8va

SPEAKER

And they shall build the old wastes, they shall raise up the former des-o-la-tions. And

they shall repair the waste ci-ties, the des-o-la-tions of ma-ny gen-er-a-tions.

(13) But thou shalt call thy walls— Sal-va-tion,— and thy gates

But thou shalt call thy walls— Sal-va-tion,— and thy gates

Praise,——— Praise,——— Praise.———

Praise,——— Praise,——— Praise.———

Moderato ♩=80

Strgs. & Org.

CHILDREN'S VOICES

Land of our birth, we pledge to thee Our love and toil in the years to be; When we are grown and take our place As men and wo-men with our race.

Fa-ther in Heav'n who lov-est

Ch⁰. all, O help thy chil - dren when they call. That they may

(15)

Ch⁰. build from age to age An un-de - filed he - ri - tage._____

SEMI CHORUS

S. Teach us the

FULL CHORUS *p*

T. Bar. Teach us the strength that can-not

FULL CHORUS *p*

B.

24

S. strength to com - fort man's dis - tress._____ Teach us de-

A. - tress._____ Teach us de-

T. Bar. - tress._____ Teach us de-

B. Teach _____

S. - light in sim - ple things, The mirth that has no bit - ter

A. - light in sim - ple things, The mirth that has no bit - ter

T. Bar. - light in sim - ple things, The mirth that has no bit - ter

B. ___ us sim - ple things, no bit - - - - - ter